HISTORY IN PICTURES

The Vietnam War

Robert Hamilton

Trans
Atlantic
Press

French Indochina

For over 1,000 years, between about 110 BC and AD 940, Vietnam was ruled by China. The collapse of the T'ang dynasty permitted a successful rebellion, which ushered in a period of independence that would endure until the end of the 14th Century. The Chinese would make repeated attempts to regain control, with varying degrees of success, until 1802, when they were expelled with the aid of the French. By 1883 however, France had claimed Vietnam as its own, and it would be subsumed into French Indochina along with Cambodia and Laos.

The First Indochina War

Resistance to French rule grew steadily into the 20th Century, and by 1941, a disaffected young man, originally named Nguyen That Thanh, had established the League for the Independence of Vietnam, or the Vietminh. By this time, he had also changed his name to Ho Chi Minh. During The Second World War, with US support, Vietminh forces defeated the Japanese in the north of the country and Ho went on to found the (largely unrecognized) Democratic Republic of Vietnam in 1945. In the south however, the British liberators returned control to the French, and within a year, skirmishes had broken out between French troops and Vietminh guerrillas that would ultimately escalate into the First Indochina War.

France attempted to reunite Vietnam under former emperor Bao Da in 1949, but having previously cooperated with both the Japanese and French, he was mistrusted by Ho's government in Hanoi. The Vietminh continued to wage war and now had the backing of the new Communist government in China. Fearful of Communist expansion in the region, the US then began to supply French forces, but despite superior technology, most notably air support, the French would be overrun by General Vo Nguyen Giap's forces at the Battle of Dien Bien Phu in 1954, bringing the conflict to a close.

A nation divided

At the Geneva Conference that followed, Vietnam was divided by a Demilitarised Zone (DMZ) along the 17th parallel, with Ho leading a Communist government in North Vietnam, and the French retaining control of South Vietnam, with a government headed by Bao Da's former Prime Minister, Ngo Dinh Diem. Reunification elections were scheduled for 1956, when the French planned to withdraw, but Diem, who had begun strengthening his position with US support, refused to participate. In response, Ho began planning to take back South Vietnam by military force.

OPPOSITE ABOVE: American GIs cautiously approach a South Vietnamese girl and woman during a search in Thuam Long for Vietcong weapons, December 1969.

RIGHT TOP: Indochinese peasants retreat towards Hanoi under the protection of French soldiers.

RIGHT MIDDLE ABOVE: French troops in an American-built amphibious vehicle manoeuvre through the swampy countryside of southern Vietnam

ABOVE: French troops scramble out of an amphibian tank and up a river bank during the hard fighting against Vietminh forces. resistance fighters parade on the esplanade of the ancient Angor Wat temple in Cambodia.

RIGHT: Female resistance fighters parade on the esplanade of the ancient Angor Wat temple in Cambodia.

Seeking out the enemy

ABOVE: Vietnamese Troops, seeking out Vietcong, move into a burning rebel village in April 1965. A few days before, units of the Vietnamese army participated in an operation to seek out and destroy the Vietcong in the area immediately West of Duc Hoa — 30 kilometers west of Saigon. The government forces pursued the elusive Vietcong through dense cane fields and inumerable streams and canals but were deprived of any knowledge of the extent of their victories due to the Vietcong habit of carrying their casualties from the battlefield.

OPPOSITE: French and colonial soldiers wade along a shallow stream in the search for Communist guerillas.

LEFT: French Legionnaires capture a Vietminh prisoner during their drive north on Thainguyen in North Indochina.

US involvement under Kennedy

After World War Two, the US had adopted a strategy of containment, in order to prevent what Presidents Truman and Eisenhower referred to as the 'domino effect', whereby the fall of one nation to Communism would trigger the fall of neighbouring states. With Castro's seizure of Cuba in 1959, and the Cuban Missile Crisis of 1962, not only was the perceived threat of Communism brought right to America's door, but the very real possibility of nuclear war with the Soviet Union ensured that a conflict against a peasant army thousands of miles away would seem a far more attractive prospect.

However, despite gains by Vietnamese Communist (Vietcong) insurgents in South Vietnam, President Kennedy was reluctant to commit troops, and instead increased financial aid and sent hundreds of military advisors, who would train the Army of the Republic of Vietnam (ARVN) in counter-insurgency.

In early 1963 however, the ARVN were defeated at the Battle of Ap Bac, and the oppressive Diem regime was becoming increasingly unpopular. This led to a Buddhist revolt that culminated in the self-immolation of a number of Buddhist priests. By November, Diem had been overthrown and executed in a coup that was effectively endorsed by the US, and just three weeks later, Kennedy himself was assassinated, to be succeeded by Lyndon B. Johnson.

ABOVE: US Army helicopters fall into tight landing formation near Phouc Vinh in war zone 'D'.

OPPOSITE: The body of a slain comrade is carried to an evacuation helicopter by soldiers of the US 1st Cavalry Division in the Ia Drang Valley early in November 1965.

LEFT: A Chinook lifts the remains of another helicopter downed by Vietcong ground fire in the An Lao Valley near Bong Son.

Operation Rolling Thunder

Throughout 1964, the political situation in South Vietnam became increasingly unstable as the North Vietnamese Army (NVA) began infiltrating the South along the 'Ho Chi Minh Trail' through neighbouring Cambodia and Laos. In response, the US began to plan attacks on the North, whilst sending more aid and personnel to the South.

By August, US-backed attacks had begun against coastal radar stations, during which the destroyer USS *Maddox* was reportedly fired upon in the Gulf of Tonkin. The incident would lead Congress to approve the Southeast Asia, or Tonkin Resolution, enabling the President to conduct military operations without a declaration of war.

Despite this, the Vietcong then stepped up their operations, attacking a number of military targets, as well as the Brinks Hotel in Saigon, finally prompting the US to launch attacks against North Vietnam. Operation Rolling Thunder, a sustained strategic bombing campaign began on March 2, 1965 and within a week, the first US ground troops had come ashore at Da Nang. By the summer, the US draft had doubled and the first major ground offensives had begun.

The Vietcong then stepped up their operations, attacking a number of military targets, as well as the Brinks Hotel in Saigon, finally prompting the US to launch attacks against North Vietnam.

BELOW: US Marine helicopters drop troops near Da Nang amid reports of Vietcong activity in the area, April 1965.

OPPOSITE TOP: US Paratroopers take two young Vietnamese girls in tow after they were captured in a Vietcong training camp near Long Bguyen, South Vietnam.

OPPOSITE BELOW: Men of the 3rd Marine Regiment's 3rd Battalion sit silently during Roman Catholic and Protestant memorial services at Da Nang Air Base for 18 Marines who died fighting near Van Tuong in August 1965.

DAILY MAIL   JUNE 10 1965

All The Way With LBJ

The United States appears to be moving inexorably into a full-scale ground war in Vietnam.

Another 2,500 American soldiers landed today at Cam Ranh Bay, 175 miles north-east of Saigon. They are engineers who will build a new port and supply depot. Their arrival came only 24 hours after it was officially announced that henceforth US troops would be committed to 'combat support' of the South Vietnamese Army. These latest reinforcements bring US military strength to 53,500 men.

President Johnson's decision to engage US troops in the coming battles clearly springs from the assessment that on its own the South Vietnamese Army would be unable to withstand the Communist assaults. The President's move marks a critical shift in US policy. After the Korean war, Presidents Eisenhower and Kennedy decided that at all cost the US must avoid involvement in a new ground war on the Asian mainland.

Within six weeks US strength is expected to rise to 70,000. And already there is talk that the numbers will reach 100,000 by the end of the summer. American strategy will be to establish a series of powerful bases along the South Vietnam coast. From them American troops will be sent into battle against the Vietcong forces.

The ground war

Initially, US troops were sent on search and destroy missions, with the intention of engaging the enemy on the battlefield in large numbers, and defeating them with superior technology. However, the NVA and Vietcong were also prepared for a war of attrition, which they would conduct with small-scale guerilla actions; employing hit-and-run tactics to frustrate and demoralise the enemy. By the end of 1966, over 380,000 US servicemen had been committed to Vietnam, with over 5,000 combat deaths and over 30,000 wounded. Most had suffered as a result of snipers, ambushes, mines and home-made booby traps, in a war where the US and their allies (which now included troops from South Korea, Australia and New Zealand), seemed to be fighting a largely invisible foe.

As a result, in early 1967, US forces began clearing huge swathes of jungle north of Saigon with bulldozers, bombs, napalm, and chemical defoliants such as Agent Orange, which would not only expose miles of Vietcong tunnel systems, but result in the deaths and forced resettlement of thousands of civilians. It was hoped that the civilian population could be physically separated from Vietcong insurgents, but by 1967, when General Nguyen Van Thieu became president in the South, it was estimated that over half the rural villages below the 17th Parallel were under Vietcong control, and towards the end of the year, the NVA began launching attacks across the DMZ.

In early 1967, US forces began clearing huge swathes of jungle north of Saigon with bulldozers, bombs, napalm, and chemical defoliants.

OPPOSITE MIDDLE: Two US soldiers stand with the wrapped body of a fallen comrade amid the smoke of a signal grenade in war zone D near Saigon.

OPPOSITE BELOW: Vietcong guerrilla suspects, blindfolded and linked arm to shoulder, are led by US infantrymen to a central interrogation point near Long Thanh.

BELOW: In scenes reminiscent of D-Day, Marines from the 7th Fleet Amphibious Ready Group storm the beach at Vung Mu.

LEFT: A lone marine sits atop Hill 881, just days after the gruelling battle for the hill had been won.

OPPOSITE ABOVE: A wounded veteran of the battle for Hill 881 is helped to a helicopter for evacuation, May 1967.

BELOW: A soldier fires at the Vietcong snipers who have just shot and wounded the man behind.

Yesterday's day-long battles shocked the US and plunged the White House into deep gloom.

Daily Mail   May 22 1966

Civil war threatens US base

South Vietnam's civil war erupted into new violence last night. Tanks and planes were thrown into a fierce battle in the northern rebel-held city of Da Nang. In Saigon police used truncheons and tear gas against Buddhist demonstrators. The rebels threatened to wreck an American air-base unless US Marines drive South Vietnam Government troops out of Da Nang.

Yesterday's day-long battles shocked the US and plunged the White House into deep gloom. Washington fears the revolt in South Vietnam's Army may grow and force America to disown Marshal Ky, the Premier.

And new Soviet threats of massive aid for North Vietnam could lead to a showdown between Russia and America.

Da Nang's worst day of terror ended last night in a 25-minute machine-gun and mortar battle. government troops, who now hold all the key points, went into action against a rebel relief column – believed to be South Vietnam's 2nd Division –marching on the city.

Government Skyraiders, making their first raid of Da Nang's civil war, strafed an advancing column and forced it back. The rebels said five of their soldiers were killed.

American Marines moved eight wounded to the pagodas where rebel troops and Buddhist monks are holding out.

ABOVE: Three UC-123 providers engage in the Vietnamese version of crop dusting - but with a difference. In this case the aircraft are spraying defoliant chemicals, harmless to human and animal life, but temporarily effective against the dense vegetation which may be shielding enemy troops from arial view. The spray increased visibility by 50 per cent within a few weeks.

OPPOSITE: Saigon, South Vietnam, September 1966. A US soldier, weighed down by his pack and a heavy roll of communications wire, rests on his rifle as his patrol stops briefly in the jungles east of Saigon. His unit was searching for a division of Vietcong believed to be nearby.

Helicopters, which were supposed to be able to land on a coin, found they couldn't touch down on the narrow hilltops of the Central Vietnam coastlands.

Fierce battles for the high ground

RIGHT: Soldiers of the US Fourth Infantry Division rest on the crest of Hill 1338 under the US flag after a fierce battle for the hill, near Dak To in November 1967.

OPPOSITE: Engineers blasted a drop area to enable a giant Chinock helicopter drop soldiers of the 5th battalion, 7th cavalry regiment to participate in Operation Thayer 11, some 15 miles southwest of Bong Son.

Casualties
from the jungle

A line of stretcher bearers brings casualties to an aid station after a US unit was attacked by Viet Cong in war Zone D about 50 miles northeast of Saigon in June 1967. 31 were killed and 113 wounded when the Americans were caught in a jungle clearing.

Battle of Khe Sanh

LEFT: Race against time: Marines carry a comrade wounded at the Battle of Khe Sanh to an evacuation helicopter. The American command in Saigon initially believed that combat operations around Khe Sanh during the summer of 1967 were just part of a series of minor North Vietnamese offensives in the border regions. That appraisal was altered when it was discovered that the People's Army of Vietnam was moving major forces into the area during the fall and winter. A build-up of Marine forces took place and actions around Khe Sanh commenced when the Marine base was isolated. During a series of desperate actions that lasted 77 days, Khe Sanh Combat Base and the hilltop outposts around it were under constant North Vietnamese ground, artillery, mortar, and rocket attacks.

ABOVE: A Wounded US Marine crawls for cover on the bridge crossing the Perfume River in Hue, January 31 1968. A bandage has been placed on his leg. The Marines were forced to give up the bridge due to heavy firing by combined Vietcong-North Vietnamese forces.

North Vietnamese Army infiltration into the South had continued to mount in 1968, as had US casualties, while social unrest had continued to grow across the US.

The Tet Offensive

By the end of 1967, the Border Battles at the DMZ had given the impression that an invasion of the South might be imminent, but US forces were completely unprepared when the Tet Offensive was launched on January 31, 1968. Breaking a ceasefire respecting the Vietnamese New Year, the NVA and Vietcong hoped to inspire a popular uprising by launching simultaneous attacks in towns and cities across the South. The US Embassy in Saigon was stormed, and battles raged for days in the streets of Saigon and Hué. When the fighting subsided, the US would claim a military victory, but the American public had seen the horrors of the offensive broadcast across the nation, and support for both the President and the war was rapidly eroding. As a result, by March, Johnson had announced that he would not be standing for another term, and by May, peace talks had begun in Paris. The negotiations quickly deadlocked, so Johnson tried to inject some momentum by announcing the cessation of Operation Rolling Thunder, during which almost a million tons of bombs had been dropped on North Vietnam with seemingly little effect. In fact, NVA infiltration into the South had continued to mount in 1968, as had US casualties, whilst social unrest had continued to grow across the US.

BELOW: A soldier runs for safety after dropping a grenade into the Vietcong bunker (seen on the left of the picture).

OPPOSITE BELOW: Marines use empty shell casings to further strengthen the fortifications around the fort of Khe Sanh near the Vietnamese border. The North Vietnamese Army attacked the fort for ten days before the start of the Tet Offensive to draw US troops away from garrisoning towns and cities in the South.

OPPOSITE ABOVE: A Marine Armoured Vehicle, armed with six recoiless guns, patrols the streets of Hue at the end of the 26-day battle for control of the city during the Tet Offensive.

DAILY MAIL   MARCH 1 1968

LBJ pours in troops

President Johnson has decided that the US war effort in Vietnam must be expanded. He has ruled out negotiations until the Allies regain the initiative in the fighting.

More troops will be sent to Vietnam as quickly as possible. The number still seems undecided but some reports say that General Westmoreland, military chief in Vietnam, has asked for 200,000. This would bring the total to 725,000. With the military manpower in the US almost exhausted, Mr Johnson has no alternative but to call up reserves.

Meanwhile American peace offers will remain officially open – but Mr Johnson has no intention of pressing them.

Saigon

US bombers struck heavily at North Vietnamese bases being enlarged to launch the first air raids on the south.

Main target was the heavily defended Vinh area, 150 miles north of the demilitarised zone. MiGs and bombers are expected to take off from Vinh to support an offensive along the border zone. Marines at Khe Sanh have been armed already with anti-aircraft weapons.

Hanoi was reported to have been bombed again today. So was the radio centre ten miles away, which controls anti-aircraft defences.

In battles last week 470 American Servicemen were killed – second only to the record 543 killed the week before. The Communists lost 5,769 dead and the South Vietnamese and other allies lost 453.

Hue

A hundred South Vietnamese soldiers and officials were found shot dead with their hands tied in caves outside Hue. This raised fears for another 200 kidnapped by the Vietcong when they held the city.

Anthony Carthew asks: But are they any good in a war like this?

There are 525,000 Americans tied up in Vietnam, but the generals say this is nowhere near enough. They say dangerous strategic gaps have appeared in the defences and the generals are right – at least in terms of the kind of war they are trying to fight here.

Since the offensive forcing the Americans and South Vietnamese to fall back on the towns and cities, there are great holes in the defensive net which was strung across the country to prevent enemy infiltration. The significant point about the way the Americans have organized their war is that, though half a million men may be serving in Vietnam, only 60,000 to 70,000 are fighting.

OPPOSITE BELOW: The 1st Brigade, 9th Infantry Division disembark from assault helicopters in rice paddies near Tan An after patrol helicopters report sighting Vietcong in the area.

ABOVE: US Marine tank crews watch the results of American air support at the perimeter of their base at Khe Sanh on March 1 1968.

BELOW: Marines help one another across a stream swollen by monsoon rains near Da Nang.

OPPOSITE BELOW: Marines at Khe Sanh use sniperscopes attached to their M-16 rifles to get a better aim at the North Vietnamese encircling their base.

RIGHT: Frightened refugees from the towns and villages around Khe Sanh shelter from North Vietnamese mortars at the American base.

OPPOSITE ABOVE: An American machine-gunner team fires as Vietcong close in on their position.

"In battles throughout the last week of February 1968, 470 American Servicemen were killed – second only to the record 543 killed the week before. The Communists lost 5,769 dead and the South Vietnamese and other allies lost 453"

A turning point as Johnson moves over

The Tet Offensive was the turning point in America's involvement in the Vietnam War. It had a profound impact on domestic support for the conflict. The offensive constituted a significant intelligence failure. On 10 May 1968, despite low expectations, peace talks began between the United States and the Democratic Republic of Vietnam. Negotiations stagnated for five months, until Johnson gave orders to halt the bombing of North Vietnam. There would soon be a new President in the US with Democratic candidate, Vice President Hubert Humphrey, running against Republican former vice president Richard Nixon. Lyndon Johnson's escalation of the war in Vietnam cost 30,000 American lives by the time he left office. His refusal to send more US troops to Vietnam was seen as Johnson's admission that the war was lost; it could not be won by escalation, at least not at a cost acceptable to the American people.

RIGHT: US soldiers return North Vietnamese fire as they are ambushed in a rubber plantation on the road between Dau Tieng and Tay Ninn. North Vietnamese troops attacked US convoys for four consecutive days in August 1968 in an attempt to protect the route southward to Saigon.

BELOW: "US soldiers move out of helicopters to begin another lightening sweep against the Vietcong who are said to be preparing for a third offensive against Saigon. Allied troops have intensified patrols and troop movement around the capital and along suspected infiltration routes in an effort to blunt any such attacks"

Within five days of his inauguration, Nixon resumed peace talks in Paris. He proposed a simultaneous withdrawal of NVA and US troops from South Vietnam.

Nixon and 'Vietnamization'

On January 20, 1969, Richard Nixon was inaugurated as the President of the United States. By March, secret bombing raids would be launched against the Ho Chi Minh Trail in Cambodia, despite the country's neutrality. Soon afterwards, the last major engagement between US and NVA troops would take place at Ap Bia, or 'Hamburger Hill', and the seemingly senseless loss of life entailed would herald not only a return to small-scale operations, but an escalation in anti-war sentiment, both in the US and amongst frontline troops.

Within five days of his inauguration, Nixon resumed peace talks in Paris. He proposed a simultaneous withdrawal of NVA and US troops from South Vietnam, but negotiations once again stalled, this time over Vietcong participation in a coalition government in the South. Nevertheless, by July the US began withdrawing troops as part of Nixon's plan for 'Vietnamization'; a gradual removal of US ground forces to allow the ARVN to take over more of the fighting. In parallel, Nixon's National Security Advisor, Henry Kissinger, began behind-the-scenes discussions with the North Vietnamese government. However, Ho Chi Minh died of a heart attack in September 1969 and was succeeded by Le Duan who pledged to continue to fight on until the US had pulled out of the war.

RIGHT: Soldiers of the First Cavalry Division descend from a Chinook helicopter into thick brush near the Cambodian border.

OPPOSITE: Troops from the 1st Air Cavalry Division search for Vietcong in the underbrush with the assistance of the agile Cayuse helicopters.

DAILY MAIL   JUNE 9 1969

Nixon pulls out 25,000 troops

America is to withdraw 25,000 combat troops from South Vietnam, President Nixon announced in Midway Island today. The withdrawal will start within 30 days and will be completed by August 31.

President Nixon spoke during a lunchtime break in his talks with President Thieu of South Vietnam. He said the Americans would be replaced by South Vietnamese troops. Further withdrawals of United States forces will be considered as conditions in Vietnam permit.

President Nixon said President Thieu had recommended the initial troop withdrawal and the US Commander in South Vietnam, General Creighton Abrams, had given his approval.

President Thieu, speaking immediately after Mr Nixon, said the withdrawal was made possible by the improvement in the South Vietnamese Armed Forces and by progress in the pacification and rural development programmes. He expressed gratitude for 'the sacrifices generously accepted by the American people in joining us in the defence of Vietnam.'

He was now confident of a 'bright and beautiful tomorrow and long-lasting peace, prosperity and brotherhood in Asia.'

President Nixon's announcement reflects optimism that the Paris peace talks, which began in May 1968, may now make some progress after months of stalemate.

America has just over 500,000 troops in South Vietnam. More than 34,000 US Servicemen have been killed there since January 1961.

DAILY MAIL   OCTOBER 16 1969

Millions in Vietnam protest

Candlelit processions and vigils closed Moratorium Day across America tonight. It was a long day of non-violent protest marred only by a few disturbances and scuffles to involve the police.

In thousands of cities, towns and hamlets it was rallies, speeches, marches, prayers – with counter-protests by the people who opposed the massive call for the ending of the Vietnam war. The demonstrations centred on the college campuses – but elementary and high schools were half empty in many parts of the nation.

Tonight ten New York theatre shows closed down, and on the stages that stayed open curtain speeches were made in support of the Moratorium. When the curtains fell, many of the actors and actresses converged on garish Times Square for a demonstration – while on Fifth Avenue the candle-bearing marchers massed at St Patrick's Cathedral.

Streets were blocked as thousands of people thronged from the rallies to new assembly points – but all was still orderly.

Mayor Lindsay, Senator Eugene McCarthy and other prominent speakers at the series of rallies ran into opposition, with some counter-demonstrators flaunting placards like 'Moratorium Day is for Commies and pigs.'

But, by and large, as the sun fell and the candles were lit, the verdict was an impressive display of non-violent protest on a scale never before known.

BELOW: An American mortar team fires 60mm shells against Vietcong in support of US marines under attack at Cua Viet.

LEFT: Placards at the ready, a group of mini-skirted girls assemble on the Victoria Embankment in London as they prepare to march on the Labour Party Headquarters to protest against the British government's support for the war in Vietnam.

In thousands of cities, towns and hamlets it was rallies, speeches, marches, prayers – with counter-protests by the people who opposed the massive call for the ending of the Vietnam war.

Daily Mail   November 21, 1969

The story that stunned America

The massacre of two Vietnamese villages is being felt here as a grave American defeat.

After 20 months of official secrecy all attempts to stifle revelations about the slaughter in My Lai and the neighbouring Son My villages broke down today. Cleveland, an American city the size of Liverpool, woke up to see the first, frightening evidence in pictures of the killings in My Lai. Their local newspaper, the Plain Dealer, was the first in the world to print pictures alleged to show the massacre.

Most of Cleveland's 800,000 people were dimly aware of reports of the massacre because the death toll was built up slowly over several days – first 30 civilians, then 109, then 300, now 567 according to the latest reports.

Terror

But not until the front page picture of scores of tangled bodies of men, women and children strewn across the ground reached them did the reports ring true. Vain attempts were made by the Army authorities last night to persuade the Plain Dealer's editor not to print pictures of the dead taken after the massacre.

The Plain Dealer printed the pictures as fact, not allegation pictures. It said nothing to suggest that their authenticity might be in doubt. One of the eight pictures showed three South Vietnamese women, one holding a little boy, cowering with terror on their faces and a small girl sheltering behind them.

The photographer, Ronald L. Haeberle, 28, an Army combat photographer, said in a page one article that moments after he took the picture the entire group was cut down. 'I noticed a woman appear from some cover and this one GI fired at her first then they all started shooting at her. I'd never seen Americans shoot civilians like that.'

Many Cleveland people refused to believe that American soldiers could be responsible for the massacre. Others were upset and angry. Mr Haeberle added in his article that as troops moved in closer to the village 'they just kept shooting at people. I remember this man distinctly, holding a small child in one arm and another child in the other walking towards us. Then all of a sudden a burst of fire and they were cut down. They were about 20ft. away. One machine-gunner did it – he opened up. There was no reaction on the guy doing the shooting. That's the part that really got me. I turned my back because I couldn't look. They opened up with two M16s. On automatic fire they went through the whole clip – 35, 40 shots. I couldn't take a picture of it, it was too much.'

Haeberle said that the attack came at 5.30 a.m. on March 16, 1968. C Company, First Battalion, 20th Infantry Regiment, 11th Light Infantry Brigade went into the hamlet of My Lai Number 4. The Number 4 indicates that there are three other villages in the district with the same name.

'No one really explained the mission, but from what I heard it was suspected that these villages were Vietcong sympathisers and it was thought there were Vietcong there.' The newspaper said that it had checked with the Adjutant General's office at Fort Benning, Georgia, that Haeberle was present in the hamlet as an Army photographer on March 16.

The My Lai revelations come at a time when President Nixon is trying to muster world opinion against Hanoi's refusal to negotiate in Paris. They are a serious blow to his attempts to persuade 'the great silent majority' of his fellow-Americans not to join the camp of the peace marchers. The Pentagon is declining comment on the incident while it is decided whether to court-martial a lieutenant for 'multiple murder.'

"No one really explained the mission, but from what I heard it was suspected that these villages were Vietcong sympathisers and it was thought there were Vietcong there"

ABOVE: A US medic works on the shattered arm of a Viet Cong prisoner who had just been discovered hiding in a bamboo thicket near Duc Pho.

OPPOSITE ABOVE: An aerial view of the destroyed Tu Cung and My Lai hamlets, where on March 16, 1968, American troops massacred Vietnamese civilians and burned the villages.

Cambodia and Laos

The conflict took a dramatic turn in March 1970, when Prince Sihanouk of Cambodia was deposed in a coup by General Lon Nol. In order to regain power, Sihanouk aligned himself with the Cambodian Communist group known as the Khmer Rouge. By appearing to have royal assent, the Khmer Rouge saw its ranks swell, prompting further US incursions into the country. This apparent widening of the conflict prompted renewed protests in the US and four demonstrators were killed at Kent State University, Ohio, when National Guardsmen opened fire with live ammunition. From then on, anti-war sentiment in the US grew dramatically and by 1971, Congress had refused funding for any operations involving US ground troops in either Cambodia or Laos. This provided the opportunity to test Nixon's 'Vietnamization' policy in the form of Operation Lam Son 719, an incursion into Laos by 17,000 ARVN troops. Despite US air support, the operation was to prove a massive failure, with the incursion force being routed, having lost almost half of their number. Nevertheless, US troop withdrawals would continue, whilst Australia and New Zealand would announce their intention to pull out of the war.

This apparent widening of the conflict prompted renewed protests in the US and four demonstrators were killed at Kent State University, Ohio, when National Guardsmen opened fire with live ammunition. From then on, anti-war sentiment in the US grew dramatically.

ABOVE: A helicopter picks up supplies to take to one of the 9th Infantry Division's forward base camps in the Mekong River Delta.

OPPOSITE: A wounded paratrooper awaits evacuation during the battle for 'Hamburger Hill' (Dong Ap Bia). Forty-six Americans and more than 500 North Vietnamese died in the battle.

DAIL MAIL   May 1, 1970

2am: US troops in Cambodia attack

American combat troops poured over the Cambodian border in a massive attack early today.

In the most momentous statement of his career President Nixon told the American people in a nation-wide TV broadcast that he had just ordered the troops to make the night assault.

The soldiers were launched against what the President described as 'the headquarters for the entire Communist military operation in South Vietnam.' They moved in after US B-52 bombers made their first raids into Cambodia.

The area of the new attack is 50 miles north of the 'Parrot's Beak' which South Vietnamese troops were attacking with a hundred or so American military 'advisers.'

President Nixon dramatically dropped all pretence that the assault on the North Vietnamese bases behind the Cambodian frontier was a South Vietnamese affair with Americans giving only support and guidance. The President announced: 'This is not an invasion of Cambodia. The areas in which these attacks will be launched are completely occupied and controlled by North Vietnamese forces. Our purpose is not to occupy the areas. Once enemy forces are driven out of these sanctuaries and their military supplies destroyed we will withdraw.'

DAILY MAIL   MAY 5, 1970

Four students shot dead in riot

Four students – two of them girls –were shot dead and 15 people injured yesterday when a college demonstration against America's invasion of Cambodia erupted into a gun battle with National Guardsmen and police. The students who died were aged 19 and 20. Three were shot in the chest and one in the head. Four of the injured are in a serious condition.

The shooting broke out at Kent State University in Ohio after National Guardsmen broke up a 300-strong rally with tear gas. Students threw stones at the troops and hurled back tear gas canisters. Then snipers fired on the Guardsmen, who opened up with M1 semi-automatics.

'The crowd was harassing them, they turned and opened fire', said Jerry Stoklas, 20, a campus newspaper photographer. 'I saw five people go down.'

A state of emergency was ordered in Kent. Guardsmen sealed off the town and a curfew was imposed. The university, scene of three days of turmoil, was closed.

Mary Hagan, a student, said: 'The troops started pelting everyone with bullets. Some of the students fell. Then a Guardsman ordered a cease-fire.' Doug McLaran, another student, said: 'I looked towards the sound of guns and saw several people wounded. I ran like hell.'

Adjutant-General Del Corso said: 'The Guard expended its entire supply of tear gas and the mob started to encircle the Guardsmen. A sniper opened fire on the troops from a rooftop and they were also hit by stones and bricks. Guardsmen facing almost certain injury and death were forced to open fire on the attackers.'

President Nixon, who last week called dissenting students 'bums,' commented: 'When dissent turns to violence it invites tragedy. I hope this tragic and unfortunate incident will strengthen the determination of all ... to stand firmly for the right of peaceful dissent and just as strongly against the resort to violence.'

A Justice Department inquiry may be ordered into the shooting.

BELOW: Sandbagged bunkers topped with canvas play home to the 4th Infantry Division at a forward camp near the Cambodian border.

OPPOSITE BELOW: Army repairman Jerry Blackston passes time before being called to duty. His job is to fix the 'People Sniffers', electrical noses that are fitted to patrol helicopters to 'sniff' out enemy hiding places. They work by picking up traces of chemical compounds unique to humans.

Nixon says it: Peace!

The Vietnam war is over. President Nixon went on nationwide television at 3 a.m. today to tell the world that America has achieved 'Peace with honour.'

The agreement initialled in Paris yesterday will effect a ceasefire throughout the war-torn country at midnight on Saturday. Within sixty days from then, said the President, all American troops will leave Vietnam and all US prisoners will be released by Hanoi.

The peace will achieve what America had fought for over so many bloody years, Mr Nixon said. 'South Vietnam has gained the right to determine its own future.'

Millions of Americans watched the Presidential broadcast, listening to the words they had waited so many years to hear. They saw Mr Nixon, calm, composed and matter of fact as he made his historic broadcast.

They saw him address himself to both North and South Vietnam in his vision of the peace to come. 'Ending the war,' he said, ' is only the first step to building the peace. All parties must now see to it that this is a peace that lasts and a peace that heals. This means that the terms of agreement must be scrupulously adhered to.

'Throughout the years of negotiations we have insisted on peace with honour,' the President said. 'In the settlement that has now been agreed to, all the stipulations I have set down have been met.'

Simultaneous announcements

As Mr Nixon spoke, simultaneous announcements were made in Hanoi and Saigon. In the South, President Thieu claimed that his refusal to accept the original peace accord last October and Mr Nixon's subsequent escalation of the bombing of the North had made a significant difference in the peace terms.

Hanoi, he said, had been forced to admit that North and South Vietnam were two separate countries and thus the sovereignty of the South was embodied into the peace agreement.

To the leaders of North Vietnam, the President pledged that the United States was prepared to make a major effort to help the country recover from the war. He said the United States would abide by the agreement but reciprocity would be needed to achieve peace.

President Nixon said: 'To the other major Powers that have been involved, even indirectly, now is the time for mutual restraint so that the peace we have achieved can last.

'Let us be proud that America did not settle for a peace that would have betrayed our ally, that would have ended the war for us but continued the war for the 50 million people of Indochina.'

In early 1972, Nixon decided to open diplomatic relations with North Vietnam's allies, China and the Soviet Union. However, by the time of his visit to Moscow, the NVA had launched a concerted effort to invade the South, which would prompt the indefinite suspension of negotiations.

Peace at hand

Back in the US, the publication of the 'Pentagon Papers', secret documents that revealed a catalogue of military and governmental transgressions, were putting the Nixon administration under further pressure to find a peaceful solution. In early 1972, Nixon decided to open diplomatic relations with North Vietnam's allies, China and the Soviet Union. However, by the time of his visit to Moscow, the NVA had launched a concerted effort to invade the South, which would prompt the indefinite suspension of negotiations, and a massive resumption of bombing in North Vietnam. By the time talks resumed, the last US ground troops had left Vietnam, and in October both the US and Hanoi governments would agree to significant concessions. Kissinger would declare, 'peace is at hand', but before the year was out, negotiations had collapsed and the bombing had begun once more.

The end in sight

By January 1973, North Vietnam had returned to the negotiating table, and on the 23rd, the Paris Peace Accords were announced. A ceasefire would begin and the US would withdraw all remaining personnel, but NVA soldiers stationed in the South would be allowed to remain. Agreements were also made regarding the exchange of POWs, and an outline put in place for a political solution in the South. The Accords were signed on the 27th, and two months later the last US troops were withdrawn. By June, in a reflection of the public mood, Congress had forbidden US military involvement in Southeast Asia, leaving the Khmer Rouge free to seize power in Cambodia, and North Vietnam poised to reclaim the South.

OPPOSITE: Battalion Commander Lt. Colonel Ardie E. McClure of the 1st Battalion 8th Cavalry Regiment calls for assistance as he evacuates Private First Class Lyle who was wounded in fighting near Bong Son.

LEFT: A South Vietnamese paratrooper wounded by a shelling attack on his unit southwest of Quang Tri waits for medics to give him an injection.

The fall of Saigon

In August 1974, Richard Nixon resigned due to the Watergate Scandal, a 'dirty tricks campaign' stemming from the 1972 presidential election. His Vice President, Gerald Ford became Commander in Chief and had to deal with resumed North Vietnamese attacks in South Vietnam. Ford would call for increased aid to Saigon in early April 1975, but by this time the NVA were advancing on the city, and the evacuation of all remaining US personnel, as well as thousands of refugees had already begun. The final evacuation, 'Operation Frequent Wind', which centred around the US Embassy, was completed on the morning of April 30, just hours before the fall of Saigon. By midday, Communist forces had made their way to the Presidential Palace, where President Minh, who had been in power for less than two days following Thieu's resignation, would make his surrender, ending the Vietnam War.

For the United States of America, the conflict had been the longest, most expensive, and least successful that the country had ever engaged in. Of the almost three million US personnel rotated through Vietnam, some 60,000 had lost their lives, whilst many of those that returned home, found themselves deeply traumatized, unwelcome, and unable to readjust to a nation that was itself damaged and divided. For the Vietnamese meanwhile, the conclusion of the war marked an end to a struggle for unification, and a fight against foreign oppression, which had persisted for centuries. The country would be officially reunited as the Socialist Republic of Vietnam on July 2, 1976.

For the United States of America, the conflict had been the longest, most expensive, and least successful that the country had ever engaged in. Of the almost three million US personnel rotated through Vietnam, some 60,000 had lost their lives.

ABOVE: Lt. Commander Mike Christian addresses a crowd during 'Mike Christian Day' April 7, 1973 in his hometown of Huntsville, Alabama. He spent six years as a North Vietnamese prisoner of war.

OPPOSITE: Sentry geese help guard the strategic Y-Bridge in Saigon. The geese acted as an early warning system for the US troops guarding the bridge, which was Saigon's main highway link to the South.

DAILY MAIL   FEBRUARY 13 1973

Goodbye Hanoi ... hello to freedom

The first group of repatriated American prisoners of war walked proudly back to freedom yesterday with smiles and waves to cheering crowds and thumbs up to television cameras to let America know they remained unbowed by their confinement in Communist camps. It was an emotion-packed homecoming for the 142 men. They walked down a long red carpet from the huge jets that had brought them from Vietnam and boarded ambulance buses for a swift ride to the military hospital where most of them will spend the next three days.There was a special cheer for Lieut.-Commander Everett Alvarez, 36, of California, who has spent almost nine years in captivity – the longest time spent by any prisoner in the North.

For 27 of the men there had been a nerve-tingling, last-minute hitch in Vietnam when a group of Vietcong prisoners refused to board their own freedom plane to Hanoi because they feared a trick. The Americans had to wait until the Communists were airborne before being whirled from Loc Ninh to Saigon by helicopter. By contrast, the release in Hanoi went like clockwork. Escort officer Lt. Col. Richard Abel said: 'When the men got off their buses, they were lined up by the ranking officer and marched to the North Vietnamese side. They didn't say anything. They stood at attention and looked straight ahead. But once aboard the planes, they embraced each other and began hugging the nurses and members of the crew. One PoW asked: "Tell me, who won the war?" He was told that South Vietnam didn't lose ... and North Vietnam didn't win.

The telephone rang in Marian Purcell's Kentucky home at 9.35 yesterday morning and the operator said 'Connecting you with the Philippines.' Then the voice she hadn't heard for nearly eight years came over crisp and clear: 'Hello Marian – how've you been?' asked her husband, Lt.-Col. Robert Purcell. Mrs Purcell, eyes swimming with tears, said: 'I saw you on TV – you were beautiful.' Another of the released men phoned the President – 'One of the most moving experiences I have had in the White House,' said Mr Nixon afterwards. Col. Robinson Risner made the call because he wanted to thank the President for his actions 'in getting us out of Vietnam.'

I watched the tanks roll in

Well, they're here. And here is no longer Saigon, the capital of an independent South Vietnam. Today it is Ho Chi Minh City, named in honour of the man who began it all 32 years ago but who died before he could see the realisation of his dream – a united, Communist Indo-China.

Now, with Cambodia under their belt and Laos half digested, that reality has come near. For those who like historical records, it was exactly 10 a.m., Wednesday.

Handshakes

An errant tank ignored the gate hurriedly opened into the presidential palace by a hopefully smiling soldier and smashed its way through the fence. A soldier on the turret fell off. The Communists had arrived.

They arrived smiling and polite. They greeted newsmen with handshakes and Saigonese with kisses. They toured hotels to ask if it were at all possible for their soldiers to be accommodated.

They sat, somewhat self-consciously, in the open-air bar on the Continental Hotel where three days ago Americans drank dry Martinis and whisky sours and sipped orange juice.

They arrived in the middle of a panic-driven frenzy of looting by South Vietnamese soldiers and civilians who smashed into Government and American warehouses. On the streets, armed soldiers were holding up the few remaining Westerners, demanding our money and our cars. Within an hour, the looting stopped.

The guns were garlanded with flowers and one puzzled clerk said: 'We were told we would be killed. It looks as if that was another lie.'

The first Communist troops to drive in looked no older than 15. Their rifles were bigger than they were. Later I saw girl soldiers – all about 17 years old – in a tank column. They were in the Vietcong uniform of black pyjamas and watched unsmiling the Saigonese who came on to the streets to greet them with white flags, cheers and laughter.

Three hours after the occupation, the victors sat on the grass-lined boulevards of this beautiful, French-inspired city, talking and making tea. Children were given lifts on the tanks. People handed the troops cigarettes and fruit. They smiled and chanted 'Victory, victory!'

After thirty years of war, this city was so happy you could actually feel the relief.

At the Palace last night the Vietcong flag – red and blue, with a gold star in the middle – fluttered from a flagpole. It was run up by a soldier as the 'two-day President,' Duong 'Big' Minh, was driven away an hour after broadcasting his surrender message. Last night he was in custody.

Pockets of resistance

There were, of course, isolated pockets of resistance. Some soldiers near the zoo saw the opposition and decided it wasn't worth it.

Another group, three miles outside the city on the Newport Bridge, were intent on a last minute redoubt. It collapsed in five minutes' fighting and some newsmen who had driven up to watch were forced from their cars by a South Vietnamese colonel who sped away in their vehicle. Apparently he hadn't worked it out that there was nowhere to go.

Salute

In the centre of Saigon, opposite the Assembly building, there is a huge monument of two soldiers, surging forward to fight the aggressor. To this, as the Communists entered, came a South Vietnamese police colonel. He saluted the statue, raised a gun to his head and pulled the trigger.

On the steps of the National Assembly Building, a Vietcong colonel said: This should be a great day for those who love peace. You will have more freedom. The curfew has been relaxed and will not begin until 6 p.m.'

At 5.55, the streets of Ho Chi Minh City were deserted. The Communists had arrived. Completely.

The victors

These are the conquerors of Saigon, the victorious troops of the North Vietnamese Army, some of them still only children. Boys of 15 in short-sleeved shirts and black strapped plastic sandals, dwarfed by the weapons they carried, marched with the units who took the city yesterday.

Girl soldiers of 15 and 17, stern and unsmiling, stood on the front of camouflaged tanks that rolled through the streets. They wore white and black silk suits, held their heads high and cradled rifles in their arms.

Yesterday the fighting was over and the Young Ones had their reward. They moved through the streets chanting 'Victory, victory' and giving clenched fist salutes. They loaded themselves with captured American-made equipment, grenades and rifles and drank picnic tea on the grass beside the roads. Their great day had come. To their nation they were the heroes of the revolution.

They loaded themselves with captured American-made equipment, grenades and rifles and drank picnic tea on the grass beside the roads. Their great day had come. To their nation they were the heroes of the revolution.

ABOVE: Chaotic scenes on the roof of the American Embassy where evacuees try to board the last flight out of Saigon, April 30, 1975. A plainclothes American punches a Vietnamese man as he tries to board the helicopter.

OPPOSITE RIGHT: A US Marine helicopter lifts off from the landing pad during the frantic US evacuation of Saigon, April 30, 1975. The 11 Marines evacuated that day were the last remaining American troops to leave Vietnam.

OPPOSITE LEFT: Evacuees scramble up the ladder to get on board one of the Air America helicopters charged with transporting Americans and foreign nationals out of Saigon and on to navy ships waiting off the coast.

RIGHT: Released prisoner of war Lt. Col. Robert L. Stirm is greeted by his family at Travis Air Force Base in Foster City, California, March 17, 1973.

This is a Transatlantic Press Book

First published in 2012

Transatlantic Press
38 Copthorne Road, Croxley Green, Hertfordshire, UK

© Atlantic Publishing
Photographs © Associated Newspapers Archive

A catalogue record for this book is available from the British Library.

ISBN 978-1-908849-08-3

Printed in China